NO
BaLONEY
ON MY
BOaT!

NO BALONEY ON MY BOAT!

MARCELLE
BIENVENU

Acadian House
PUBLISHING
LAFAYETTE, LOUISIANA

Copyright © 2011 by Marcelle Bienvenu

Library of Congress Cataloging-in-Publication Data

Bienvenu, Marcelle.
  No baloney on my boat! : recipes to be enjoyed in the great outdoors / Marcelle Bienvenu.
     p. cm.
  Includes indexes.
  ISBN-13: 978-0-925417-69-5 (hardcover)
  ISBN-10: 0-925417-69-6 (hardcover)
  1. Cooking on ships. 2. Ready meals. 3. Outdoor cooking. I. Title.

  TX840.M7B54 2011
  641.5'78--dc22

                        2011009536

♦ Published by Acadian House Publishing, Lafayette, Louisiana (Edited by Trent Angers; produced by Jon Russo and Angelina Leger)

♦ Cover design and interior illustrations by Angelina Leger, Lafayette, Louisiana

♦ Cover photo of the author by Mickey Delcambre, New Iberia, Louisiana

♦ Printed by Walsworth Print Group, Marceline, Missouri

*To my parents, who taught me to enjoy and appreciate
the waterways that abound in Louisiana, and who
instilled in me a sense of adventure
and love of good food*

*And to Babs and all the friends who have
invited me and my husband to enjoy their
boats – from the "Lucky Baby," a
restored 16-foot Boston Whaler,
to "The Adventurer," a
96-foot Burger yacht*

EATING WELL IN THE GREAT OUTDOORS

Baloney sandwiches... Spam on white bread... Vienna sausage with crackers... and maybe a few Moon Pies.

These are some of the foods that we grab and throw into the truck when we're going fishing, hunting or camping. It's what many of us have eaten for generations while enjoying life in the great outdoors.

But renowned cookbook author Marcelle Bienvenu has a better idea. She points out that there are lots of tasty and nutritious foods that can be prepared either in advance of or during our outdoors adventures.

And the baloney sandwich isn't one of them.

No, sir, there will be no baloney on Marcelle's boat – or at her campsite or beach party either!

So, she's written this cookbook to provide a more nutritious alternative.

It's filled with recipes that are easy to prepare. They can be made before you leave home, or they can be prepared at the camp, at the beach-house, or on the boat (if it's equipped for cooking – which many boats are these days).

The recipes are ideal for fishing trips, hunting trips, camping trips, picnics, beach parties and patio events.

In addition to the recipes, you'll find a smattering of useful tips in the pages of this book – how to stock your pantry, which utensils to bring along, how to pack prepared foods most efficiently, foods that must be kept on ice, etc.

In this day and age – with the help of this little cookbook – there's just no good reason to stay married to the baloney sandwich while enjoying the great outdoors.

– Trent Angers,
Editor

Acknowledgements

I would like to thank Babs Grant for giving me the inspiration for the name of this cookbook when she showed me how easy it was to prepare enjoyable meals on her boat.

I must also thank Adele and Bud Forrest, with whom my husband and I shared many good times aboard their sailboat, "Island Time," and who always kept us well fed.

Many thanks go to Karen Peery and her husband Captain Dick Peery, who cooked and served us elegant meals aboard "The Adventurer."

And, of course, I will always be indebted to my husband and our many friends who constantly support me in all my endeavors.

My gratitude also goes out to Trent Angers and his staff at Acadian House Publishing for all their hard work.

And finally to my family, who are always encouraging me to continue my adventures in life, many thanks.

– M.B.

CONTENTS

NO BALONEY ON MY BOAT!

THE DAYS OF THE BALONEY SANDWICH ARE NUMBERED!

THE INSPIRATION FOR THIS BOOK WAS two-fold.

When we were youngsters, my parents often took me and my siblings on day trips on our 20-foot aluminum boat (Ouch, the seats were hot!). Sometimes we launched the boat at Catahoula Lake near the Atchafalaya Spillway in southern Louisiana for a fishing trip. Other times we put the boat in at Vermilion Bay for an excursion to Marsh Island to fish and maybe catch a few shrimp and crabs for an evening meal.

Before Papa started his old Evinrude motor, he checked his list: bait, rods and reels, ice chest filled with red pops buried in crushed ice, a pound of bologna, a loaf of Evangeline Maid bread, one dozen hard-boiled eggs sprinkled with salt and black pepper and packed in an airtight container, two tins of sardines, a few cans of Vienna sausage, and a sleeve or two of Saltine crackers. We would not leave the dock until all was accounted for.

It was a ritual that was repeated often. When my brothers became young men with their own boats, they adopted the procedure.

One summer when my Baby Brother Bruce and his wife Nancy invited us to join them on their 30-foot boat for an excursion from Lake Charles, Louisiana, to Galveston, Texas, via the Intracoastal Canal, I offered to supply the makings for our luncheon stop near the Sabine River. They accepted my offer. When we were loading up the boat, Bruce got his check list out and began checking off Papa's items.

"Stop, I have everything for lunch packed in my ice chest!" I yelled.

He replied deadpan:

"We cannot leave the dock unless I have my bologna and white bread. I don't care what you have brought along."

When we stopped for our lunch break, I pulled out a large jug of chilled gazpacho soup made with garden-grown tomatoes, sandwiches stacked with thinly sliced medium-rare beef tenderloin and dressed with a mixture of mayonnaise and Creole mustard, and a container of strawberries, blackberries and blueberries splashed with rum and tweaked with fresh mint leaves.

Bruce took one look at the layout on the colorful tablecloth I had brought along and spread on the small folding table in the cabin of the boat.

"This looks like something out of *Southern Living*. Where are my bologna sandwiches?" he blurted out.

We did manage to cajole him into trying the food, and he had to admit it was pretty darn good. But he swore that it was bad luck not to have bologna onboard and that our dearly departed Papa was going to come and pinch our toes in the middle of the night for not keeping to tradition.

Not too long after that, my husband Rock and I had occasion to join Richard Grant and his then-wife Babs on their restored Hatteras, "The Sundance," for a fishing trip starting at Venice, Louisiana, and venturing out into the deep waters of the Gulf of Mexico. During three days onboard, I never saw or ate anything that resembled a bologna sandwich, sardines or Vienna sausage.

With a little preparation and ingenuity, Babs regaled us with pre-made sausage cake for breakfast, *ceviche* made with tuna (caught on our fishing trip) for a late evening dinner, and summer spaghetti for a quick lunch.

I was so intrigued I began filling a file folder with her suggestions and some ideas of my own. Now, I'm prepared for just about any boating expedition, whether on our party barge cruising on Bayou Teche, on a friend's sleek 42-foot sailboat, on large fishing boats or even in a canoe on the bayou. It's all about adapting to the situation.

There is no reason to be on the water, whether it be a bayou, river, lake or even the high seas, armed with soggy bologna sandwiches or smashed deviled eggs. Of course, there are those rough and ready guys who are as happy as clams with that – but just as likely there are those who would like to enjoy a more enticing menu.

Mega-yachts can boast of fully equipped galleys with enough space to stow plenty of pantry items. Some boats may have a two-burner stove, an under-counter refrigerator, and even a small microwave. Smaller boats can accommodate only an ice chest or two.

No matter what size vessel you have, you should be able to enjoy onboard delights. It just takes a little planning, some imagination and creativity, and a sense of adventure.

AS THE BOY SCOUTS SAY, 'BE PREPARED'

Y OU ARE THE ONLY ONE WHO CAN determine what foods, if any, you can prepare onboard your boat. What size cooler do you have? Or does your boat have a little refrigerator? Do you have space to store canned goods? Know the limitations.

Study the recipes. Plan a couple of menus you *think* you like. Can they be prepared in the space that's available to you? Like a Boy Scout, be prepared. Don't try to offer a four-course meal before you have tested the recipes.

If you'll be docking at a marina, find out as much about it as you can beforehand so you'll know what to expect. For example, some marinas allow dockside cooking and some even provide grills just a few steps from your boat slip.

Investigate the possibilities of attaching a small grill to your watercraft. Visit your local marine supply store as well as places like Cabela's and Bass Pro Shop. These stores have all types of portable cook-tops and grills, storage containers, and a plethora of other items from which to choose.

The marina may have a store that supplies not only bait and ice, but also perishable items like bread, dairy products and even fresh fruit and vegetables.

On a boating trip in the Bahamas, I noticed fishermen cleaning their catch at a fish-cleaning area at the marina. I sidled up to one of the guys and asked if he was willing to part with some of his fish – cleaned, of course. Before I could make a cash offer, he offered me four pounds of fish, ready to cook, in exchange for a few cold beers. Easy enough.

If your marina has a town nearby, venture forth and look into the possibility that there may be a fishmonger, a bakery, a farmers' market or gourmet shops, which can supply you with local seafood, cheeses, other delicacies and beverages.

Stock up on disposable plates, utensils, napkins and cups if you have enough storage space. But remember, you'll have to dispose of your trash properly when you get ashore. If space allows and you are able to wash your dishes, by all means invest in boat-friendly, non-breakable dinnerware, eating utensils, wine glasses and tumblers. You may even want to splurge on some colorful, nautical-themed fabric napkins to have on hand for special occasions.

WHAT TO BRING?
The possibilities are (almost) endless

SEASONAL INGREDIENTS OR WHAT YOU have stashed in your freezer or refrigerator can inspire the menu.

A chunk of cheese or leftover pork roast is ideal for putting on bread slathered with Dijon mustard. Fig preserves can be plopped on a slice of pound cake. Blue cheese, fresh pears and ginger snap cookies are a great combination to bring along. Pickles that you put up last summer are ideal for munching. Flavor plain tea with mint or lime. A bottle of wine is always nice, as is cold, cold beer.

There are many items that can be brought along depending on your boat capacity.

Assorted deli meats and cheeses are always a good bet for sandwiches. Don't forget breads and rolls as well as condiments such as mustard and mayonnaise.

A baked ham goes a long way. It's great for sandwiches, and small cubes of it can be added to salads for a chef's salad. (Use whatever is on hand to make this: lettuce, chunks of cheese, marinated vegetables, olives, cherry tomatoes.) Bring along a couple of salad dressings.

While I am a big believer in fresh ingredients, canned goods come in handy onboard if you can accommodate them. Canned sliced beets are great to add to salads; the same is true of canned white and/or green asparagus, artichoke hearts, hearts of palm, and pickled mushrooms. Breakfast items such as muffins come in all sizes and flavors. You'll find beverages in one-serving-size bottles or cans. Snack items like trail mixes, cookies and dried fruit come in small packages as well.

Take some time to peruse your supermarket. You'll find a wealth of items ideal for all kinds of outings.

Instant potatoes, dry soup mixes, and instant grits are easy to store – just add water and you're good to go.

Oh, and don't forget to pack salt and pepper; travel sizes are available at supermarkets. Tabasco or other hot sauces, sugar packets and sugar substitutes, dry coffee creamer, coffee, tea and lemonade or ice tea mix can be packed in airtight containers.

Small cans of cut green beans, corn (shoepeg), artichoke hearts and peas can be used for salads. Toss them with a bit of salad dressing for an added flavor. Canned tuna is always a good bet. Mix it with Mil's Mayonnaise (see recipe, page 74) to dress it up.

FOOD SAFETY

BEFORE WE EMBARK ON OUR GREAT adventure, I must impress upon you that it's very important to keep perishable foods either in a refrigerator or iced down in secured containers.

I have a collection of wide-mouthed, non-breakable containers with screw-tops, which are ideal for storing cold soups, marinated vegetables, mint tea and lemonade, and other cold items. At large discount centers, you can purchase all manner of airtight containers in which to store food. Investigate travel containers that accommodate both hot and cold foods for short-term storage. There are many insulated containers of all shapes and sizes to fit your needs.

Do not leave food out on the counter once the meal is completed. Bring a good supply of plastic storage bags and small containers with lids that can easily accommodate leftovers and will stow properly. Ice packs that can be frozen are ideal for day trips.

My Baby Brother Bruce fills plastic bottles of all sizes with water and stores them in his home freezer. They are ideal for stashing in ice chests as they melt much slower than crushed ice. And, speaking of crushed ice, it's still fairly inexpensive. So, don't be stingy: Keep your ice chests packed with bags of ice.

BREAKFAST

Crunchy Breakfast Bread

Makes 1 loaf

- 1 ¾ cups of all-purpose flour
- 2 ½ teaspoons of baking powder
- ½ teaspoon of salt
- 1 cup of sugar
- ¾ cup of nutlike cereal nuggets
- 1 large egg, lightly beaten
- ½ cup of raisins
- 2 tablespoons of grated orange rind
- 1 cup of milk
- ¼ cup of vegetable oil

Combine the flour, baking powder, salt, sugar, and cereal in a large bowl. Make a well in the center of the mixture. Combine the egg and remaining ingredients and add to the dry ingredients, stirring just until moistened.

Spoon the mixture into a greased and floured 8½ x 4½ x 3-inch loaf pan.

Bake at 350 degrees for one hour. Cool in the pan on a wire rack for 10 minutes. Remove the loaf and cool completely on a wire rack before wrapping in foil.

Cranberry Fruit–Nut Bread

Makes 1 loaf

A great breakfast item, it can also be sliced to use to make ham sandwiches.

- 2 cups of all-purpose flour
- 1 cup of sugar
- 1 1/2 teaspoons of baking powder
- 1 teaspoon of salt
- 1/2 teaspoon of baking soda
- 2 tablespoons of vegetable oil
- 3/4 cup of fresh orange juice
- 1 egg, well beaten
- 1 tablespoon of orange peel
- 1 1/2 cups of fresh cranberries, coarsely chopped
- 1/2 cup of chopped pecans or walnuts

Preheat the oven to 350 degrees. Generously grease and lightly flour a 9x5x3-inch loaf pan. (You can also do this in muffin tins.)

In a bowl, **mix** together the flour, sugar, baking powder, salt and baking soda. Stir in the vegetable oil. Stir in the orange juice, egg and orange peel, mixing just to moisten. Fold in the cranberries and the nuts. Spoon mixture into the prepared pan.

Bake one hour or until a wooden toothpick inserted in the center comes out clean.

Cool on a rack for 15 minutes. Remove the loaf from the pan and cool completely before wrapping in foil.

Southern Sausage Cake

Makes about 8 servings (Freezes well)

This can be prepared in advance in a disposable 9x9x2-inch baking tin, and either frozen or refrigerated until time to be served. As it is best slightly warm or at room temperature, it's usually best to take it out ahead of time. It's a good breakfast item, but it certainly is appropriate for a snack or appetizer with cocktails.

- 1 pound of hot bulk sausage
- 1/2 cup of chopped onions
- 1 cup of chopped red bell peppers
- 1 cup of chopped green bell peppers
- 1/4 cup of grated Parmesan cheese
- 1/2 cup of grated Velveeta cheese
- 1 egg, slightly beaten
- 1/4 teaspoon of Tabasco sauce
- 1/2 teaspoon of Cajun or Creole seasoning (I use Tony Chachere's.)
- 2 cups of Bisquick
- 3/4 cup of milk
- 1/4 cup of sour cream

Preheat the oven to 350 degrees.

Cook the sausage in a skillet over medium heat. As the sausage begins to brown, add the onions and bell peppers and cook until soft, 3 to 4 minutes.

Remove from the heat and drain off excess fat.

Add the cheeses, egg, Tabasco sauce and seasoning. Mix well.

Make a batter with the Bisquick, milk and sour cream in a large mixing bowl. Gently stir in the sausage mixture, then spoon into a lightly greased disposable 9x9x2-inch baking tin, spreading evenly.

Bake until browned, 25 to 30 minutes.

Cool before storing in an airtight container to freeze or refrigerate. When ready to serve, cut into squares.

Note: Bisquick is also handy for making biscuits and pancakes. Store it in an airtight container on your vessel.

Banana-Nut Bread

Makes 8 to 10 servings

- 3 medium bananas, mashed
- ½ cup of cooking oil
- 2 eggs
- 1 cup of sugar
- 1 ½ cups of flour
- 1 teaspoon of baking soda
- ¼ teaspoon of salt
- 1 teaspoon of vanilla
- ½ cup of chopped pecans or walnuts

Preheat the oven to 350 degrees. Liberally grease a loaf pan.

In a large bowl, **combine** all the ingredients until mixed thoroughly. Do not overmix. Pour mixture into the pan and bake for 1 hour and 15 minutes, or until a toothpick inserted in the center comes out clean.

Turn out on a rack and cool before slicing.

Bacon–Cheese Bread

Makes 1 loaf

- 1 ½ cups of all-purpose flour
- ⅓ cup of sugar
- 2 teaspoons of baking powder
- ½ teaspoon of baking soda
- ½ teaspoon of salt
- 1 cup (4 ounces) of shredded sharp Cheddar cheese
- ¾ cup of quick-cooking oats
- 6 slices of bacon, cooked and crumbled
- 2 eggs, beaten
- ½ cup of milk
- ¼ cup of vegetable oil

Combine the flour, sugar, baking powder, baking soda, salt, cheese, oats and bacon in a large bowl. Set aside.

Combine the eggs, milk and oil in another bowl and add to the first mixture, stirring just enough to moisten the dry ingredients.

Spoon the batter into a greased and floured 8½ x 4½ x 3-inch loaf pan.

Bake at 350 degrees for 35 to 40 minutes or until a wooden toothpick inserted in the center of the bread comes out clean. Let bread cool for 10 minutes before wrapping in foil.

Zucchini Bread

Makes 2 loaves

- 3 tablespoons of butter
- 3 eggs
- 1 ¼ cups of vegetable oil
- 1 ½ cups of sugar
- 2 teaspoons of vanilla extract
- 2 cups of grated raw zucchini (unpeeled)
- 2 cups of all-purpose flour
- 2 teaspoons of baking soda
- 1 teaspoon of baking powder
- 1 teaspoon of salt
- 2 teaspoons of ground cinnamon
- 2 teaspoons of ground cloves
- 2 teaspoons of grated nutmeg
- 2 teaspoons of ground ginger
- 1 cup of chopped pecans or walnuts

Preheat the oven to 350 degrees. Lightly butter two loaf pans.

Beat the butter, eggs, oil, sugar and vanilla in a large mixing bowl until light and thick. Fold in the zucchini.

Sift together all the dry ingredients and fold in to the zucchini mixture.

Add the nuts and pour the mixture into the prepared pans.

Bake until a tester inserted in the bread comes out clean, about 1 hour and 15 minutes. Remove the loaf from the oven and cool a bit in the pans before turning out on a wire rack to cool longer.

The bread can be served warm or at room temperature.

Strawberry Bread

Makes 2 loaves

- 3 cups of all-purpose flour
- 2 cups of sugar
- 1 teaspoon of baking soda
- 1 teaspoon of salt
- 1 teaspoon of ground cinnamon
- 4 eggs, beaten
- 1 ¼ cups of vegetable oil
- 2 (10-ounce) packages of frozen strawberries, thawed and chopped

Combine the flour, sugar, baking soda, salt and cinnamon in a large mixing bowl. Make a well in the center of the mixture.

Combine the remaining ingredients and add to the dry ingredients, stirring until well mixed.

Spoon the mixture into two greased and floured 9x5x3-inch loaf pans. Bake at 350 degrees for one hour.

Cool loaves in pans for 10 minutes. Remove from the pans and let cool completely on wire racks.

APPETIZERS
& SNACKS

THE COCKTAIL HOUR

After a long, hot day on the water – whether it be spent fishing, cruising or exploring – the cocktail hour is always welcome. Moored "on the hook" or in a marina, refreshing drinks and an array of snacks can be assembled easily.

Bring along assorted cheeses and crackers, a variety of nuts, pickled okra and assorted olives. Tins of smoked oysters and sardines as well as a pack of smoked salmon can be packed easily onboard. Serve with Dijon mustard or cream cheese on crackers.

Heartier fare can also serve as a light supper.

Antipasto

Makes about 4 appetizer servings

Antipasto means "before the meal" and is often served as a first course to many Italian meals. Traditional antipasto includes cured meats, olives, roasted garlic, cheeses, marinated peppers and mushrooms. You can create your own with very little preparation. It can be served with toasted croutons, which you can make before you leave home, and stored in an airtight container or storage bags.

- 1 (6-ounce) jar of marinated artichoke hearts (Do not drain.)
- 1 (14-ounce) can of hearts of palm, sliced and drained
- 1 (3 1/4-ounce) can of sliced ripe or cured olives, drained
- 1 small jar of marinated mushrooms (Do not drain.)
- 1/4 cup of thinly sliced summer sausage

Combine all the ingredients and store in an airtight container in the refrigerator or ice chest.

Marinated Shrimp & Corn

Makes 6 servings

Store this dish in a large, wide-mouth Plexiglass container and bring it along in the ice chest.

- ¾ cup of olive oil
- ½ cup of red wine vinegar
- 3 tablespoons of Creole mustard
- 2 tablespoons of chopped chives or green onions
- 2 tablespoons of chopped fresh parsley
- 2 pounds of large shrimp, cooked in seasoned water, then peeled and deveined
- 2 cups of fresh corn kernels
- Salt and freshly ground black pepper, to taste

Combine the oil, vinegar, mustard, green onions and parsley in a mixing bowl. Whisk to blend and set aside.

Cool the shrimp after they are cooked and peeled.

Steam the corn kernels in a little water for about two minutes. Remove from the heat, drain and cool.

Put the shrimp and corn in a large shallow glass bowl. Pour in the marinade and toss to coat evenly. Season with salt and black pepper.

Cover and chill for four hours before transferring the mixture to a wide-mouth Plexiglass container that can be stored onboard in an ice chest or refrigerator.

Chicken Liver *Paté*

Makes about 24 appetizer portions

Of course, this is a great hors d'oeuvre to bring along.
Make it in advance and store it in an airtight container.
Pack some crackers or toasted slices of French bread and
you're good to go!

- **3 tablespoons of butter**
- **¼ cup of finely chopped onions**
- **1 ½ pounds of chicken livers, cleaned**
- **2 hard-boiled egg yolks**
- **4 tablespoons of softened butter**
- **½ cup of heavy cream**
- **⅓ cup of Cognac**
- **¼ teaspoon of grated nutmeg**
- **Salt and freshly ground black pepper, to taste**
- **1 tablespoon of chopped green onions or fresh chives**

Heat 3 tablespoons of the butter in a skillet over medium heat. Add the onions and cook, stirring, for 2 to 3 minutes. Add the chicken livers and cook just until the pink disappears. Remove from the heat.

Purée the mixture in a blender or food processor until smooth. Press the egg yolks through a sieve and add to the liver mixture together with the 4 tablespoons of softened butter, the cream, Cognac, nutmeg, salt and pepper. Process to mix well.

Spoon the *paté* into a decorative bowl, cover it, and chill for several hours.

Sprinkle the top of the *paté* with the green onions or chives before serving with toast points or crackers.

Seafood Spread

Makes about 20 appetizer portions

I'm a big fan of spreads. This one can be served on crackers or toasted bread or on slices of tomatoes or cucumbers. While this is great to serve as an appetizer, you can certainly use it for a quick lunch or supper. Spread it on the bread of your choice for a great sandwich. (Since it contains mayonnaise, be sure it is kept well chilled.)

- 2 cups of finely chopped cooked lobster, shrimp or crawfish tails
- 1 cup of finely chopped celery
- ½ cup of finely chopped green onions
- ¼ cup of finely chopped red bell peppers
- 1 cup of mayonnaise
- 3 tablespoons of fresh lemon juice
- 1 tablespoon of capers
- ¼ teaspoon of salt
- ⅛ teaspoon of freshly ground black pepper
- ⅛ teaspoon of Tabasco sauce
- 1 tablespoon of finely chopped parsley

Combine all of the ingredients in a mixing bowl and stir to mix well. Chill for at least two hours before serving.

Serve with party crackers or toasted pita bread triangles.

Herbed Cheese Spread

Makes about 20 appetizer portions

Make this spread ahead of time and keep it chilled. It's great to spread on party crackers to serve during the cocktail hour onboard.

- ½ cup of crème fraîche
- 4 ounces of cream cheese at room temperature
- 1 teaspoon of chopped fresh thyme
- 1 tablespoon of chopped fresh parsley
- Pinch of cayenne
- 1 teaspoon of fresh lemon juice

Whip the crème fraîche in an electric mixer until fluffy and set aside.

In a separate bowl, **whip** the cream cheese with the remaining ingredients until light and fluffy.

Fold in the whipped crème fraîche and refrigerate until ready to use.

DEVILED EGGS OF ALL KINDS

Deviled eggs are a favorite of mine anytime and anywhere!

I like them especially when I'm out on the water. Once they are made, I put two halves together and wrap them individually in plastic wrap then store them in an airtight container to put in the cooler or refrigerator. They don't look pretty, but they taste heavenly!

Oh, if you want a firmer filling, add about two tablespoons of softened butter to the hard-boiled egg yolk mixture while mixing in a food processor.

You can be creative here! Use crabmeat or chopped boiled shrimp. I love topping the eggs with a bit of caviar when I have some on hand. Hey, I've even added a teaspoon or two of potted meat or crumbled bacon bits. Chopped black or green olives are great! A spoonful of canned tuna is not bad either.

Pimento Deviled Eggs

Makes 1 dozen

- 6 hard-cooked eggs, peeled, cut in half and yolks mashed in a bowl
- ¼ cup of finely shredded sharp Cheddar cheese
- 1 tablespoon plus 1 teaspoon of canned drained and chopped pimentos
- 2 tablespoons of mayonnaise
- 2 teaspoons of Dijon mustard
- 2 teaspoons of chopped Vidalia onions or other sweet onions
- ½ teaspoon of grated garlic
- Salt and pepper, to taste
- Chopped pimentos for garnish

Combine the thoroughly mashed yolks with the cheese, pimentos, mayonnaise, mustard, onion and garlic. (This can be done in a food processor.) Taste, then season with salt and pepper.

Fill the whites evenly with the mixture and garnish with chopped pimentos.

Spicy Deviled Eggs

Makes 2 dozen

- **12 hard-boiled eggs**
- **½ cup of mayonnaise**
- **2 teaspoons of Dijon mustard**
- **1 teaspoon of sweet pickle relish**
- **½ teaspoon of minced jalapeño peppers**
- **½ teaspoon of Tabasco sauce**
- **1 ½ teaspoons of Creole or Cajun seasoning mix**
- **Minced parsley for garnish**

Slice the eggs in half lengthwise and remove the yolks. Set aside the whites.

Combine the yolks and the remaining ingredients in a food processor, and pulse several times to make a smooth mixture.

Spoon equal amounts of the mixture into the egg whites.

Cover and **chill** for at least one hour before serving. When ready to serve, sprinkle with the parsley.

Smoked Oyster Log

Makes 1 log to serve 12 to 14 appetizers

Make this dish ahead of time and store in an airtight container so you can put it into your ice chest or onboard refrigerator.

- 1 (8-ounce) package of cream cheese, softened
- 2 tablespoons of mayonnaise
- 1 teaspoon of Worcestershire sauce
- Salt, cayenne and Tabasco pepper sauce, to taste
- ½ teaspoon of minced garlic
- 1 tin of smoked oysters, drained and chopped
- 2 tablespoons of minced parsley

Combine the cream cheese and mayonnaise and blend well. Add the Worcestershire, salt, cayenne and Tabasco. Stir in the garlic and smoked oysters. Blend well.

Wrap the mixture in wax paper and chill for at least 30 minutes.

Shape the chilled mixture into a log and roll it in the parsley to coat evenly.

Serve with party crackers.

Pico de Gallo

Makes about 2 cups

This is great to serve with corn chips or tortilla chips, and for dressing fajitas. I also like it spooned on grilled steaks or chicken breasts during the summer. This can be made before you leave shore and stored in an airtight container, chilled. The great thing is that the longer it sits, the better it tastes. It will keep for as long as a week.

- 2 cups of diced ripe tomatoes (or canned diced tomatoes)
- 1/2 cup of finely chopped red onions
- 1/4 cup of thin strips of fresh basil
- 2 tablespoon of chopped fresh cilantro
- 3 tablespoons of fresh lime juice
- 1 teaspoon (or more, to taste) of chopped pickled jalapeños
- 1 teaspoon of balsamic or apple cider vinegar
- Salt and freshly ground black pepper, to taste
- Tabasco sauce, to taste

Combine all the ingredients in an airtight container and chill for at least 30 minutes before serving.

Roasted Red Pepper Dip

Makes 1 ¼ cups

A pleasant change from guacamole, this dip has the color and taste to complement crudités, toasted pita bread triangles, or crisp crackers. It can be made ahead of time and stored in an airtight container on ice.

- 2 red bell peppers
- 3 slices of white bread, crusts removed
- ¼ cup of milk
- ¼ cup of pitted green olives
- 1 clove of garlic
- 2 tablespoons of olive oil
- 1 tablespoon of fresh lemon juice
- ½ teaspoon of Tabasco pepper sauce
- Sliced green olives for garnish

Preheat the broiler.

Slice the peppers in half lengthwise, then core and seed. Lay the pepper slices skin side up in a shallow broiling pan and set the pan 3 inches below the heat.

Broil the peppers until the skin blisters and turns black. Transfer the peppers to a plastic bag and close it; let them steam for 15 minutes. When they are cool enough to handle, peel off the skin.

Meanwhile, **break** the bread and place it in a small bowl, add the milk, and soak for 10 minutes.

Combine the bread, peppers, olives and garlic in a food processor and process with a pulsing motion for about 4 seconds.

Add the oil, lemon juice and Tabasco sauce, and pulse 3 seconds longer.

Spoon the dip into a serving bowl, cover, and let stand at least 30 minutes to blend the flavors.

Garnish with sliced olives.

Jezebel Sauce (No. 1)

Makes 3 jars

This is a recipe from Karen Peery, the cook on "The Adventurer," a yacht owned by friends of mine. She says:

"This is an old Southern recipe handed down over the years. Makes three jars and can be refrigerated for several months – and also makes a good pass-on gift."

She won second prize in the appetizer division in the Grand Marnier Charteryacht League Cookoff for this by putting a little Grand Marnier in it.

- 1 (8- to 10-ounce) jar of apple jelly
- 1 (8- to 10-ounce) jar of apricot preserves
- 1 (2-ounce) can of Coleman's Mustard
- 1 small jar of prepared horseradish

Mix all ingredients together and divide into 3 sterilized jars; use one over cream cheese with crackers and save two for another time.

When **serving**, Karen suggests garnishing the cream cheese and Jezebel Sauce with strips of red pepper to make it attractive.

Jezebel Sauce (No. 2)

Makes 3 cups

Just about every Southern state claims the origin of this wonderful tangy sauce. I was introduced to it by my friend Mary Forest McEnery Broussard, and I have several recipes – all good. Most people serve it over cream cheese to serve with crackers, but I also like it dabbed on cold baked chicken, ham, pork or beef.

- 1 cup of apple jelly
- 1 cup of pineapple-orange marmalade or pineapple preserves
- 1 (6-ounce) jar of prepared mustard
- 1 (5-ounce) jar of prepared horseradish
- ¼ teaspoon of freshly ground black pepper

Beat the apple jelly in a mixing bowl at medium speed with an electric mixer until smooth. Add the remaining ingredients and beat at medium speed until blended. Chill.

Spinach Bread

Makes 8 to 10 servings

- 4 tablespoons of butter
- 3 eggs
- 1 cup of all-purpose flour
- 1 teaspoon of salt
- 1 teaspoon of baking powder
- 1 cup of milk
- 1 teaspoon of chopped dill
- 4 cups of cleaned and chopped fresh spinach
- 1 pound of grated Monterey Jack cheese

Melt the butter in a 9½ x 13 x 2-inch baking pan in a 375-degree oven.

In a mixing bowl, **beat** the eggs and add the flour, salt, baking powder, milk and dill. Mix well.

Add the spinach and three-fourths of the cheese. Mix well.

Spread the mixture over the butter in the baking pan. Sprinkle the top of the mixture with the remaining cheese.

Bake uncovered for 30 minutes at 375 degrees.

Remove from the oven and cool for several minutes before cutting into squares.

Sausage-Stuffed Loaves

Makes about 36 appetizer portions

If your boat has an oven, these can be made ahead of time, wrapped in foil and frozen, then warmed onboard.

- 2 fat, long loaves of French bread
- 8 ounces of bulk sausage
- 8 ounces of ground beef chuck
- 1 cup of chopped onions
- 1 egg
- 1 teaspoon of Creole mustard
- ¼ cup of chopped parsley
- Salt and freshly ground black pepper, to taste
- 2 tablespoons of butter
- 2 cloves of garlic, mashed

Cut off the ends of the loaves and hollow out the loaves with your fingers. Pulse the soft bread in a food processor to make coarse crumbs. Reserve the bread ends.

Brown the sausage in a heavy skillet over medium heat. Add the beef and onions and cook until the beef is browned.

Combine the bread crumbs, meat mixture, egg, mustard, parsley, salt and pepper in a large mixing bowl.

Spoon the mixture into the bread shells and attach the bread ends with small skewers.

Melt the butter over medium heat and stir in the garlic. Cook, stirring, for about 30 seconds. Brush the loaves with the garlic-butter and wrap in aluminum foil. (The loaves can be frozen at this point.)

When ready to **heat**, allow loaves to thaw, then open the foil slightly on top and bake at 350 degrees for about 20 minutes or until heated through.

Cut into 1-inch slices for *hors d'oeuvres* or cut each loaf into four pieces for main-course servings.

Ceviche

Makes 8 to 10 servings

Ceviche (also spelled as cebiche or seviche) is citrus-marinated seafood. Some say it may have originated in Polynesia, while others claim it may have been developed by the Spanish in Latin America.

You can use just about any kind of seafood – shellfish, fish, conch – but it must be fresh. Think scallops, shrimp, bite-size chunks of tuna, salmon or conch. Heck, put a little of each; use what is available.

The juice of limes, oranges and lemons is the acid that "cooks" the seafood. There are many combinations so you can be creative and use what pleases your taste buds. You can add chopped fresh tomatoes or canned diced ones. Fresh herbs are more flavorful, but you can certainly use dried ones as well.

You can make the marinade mixture in advance and store it in an airtight container in the refrigerator or ice chest for as long as two days. Simply add the seafood and chill for as little as 6 hours or as much as 24 hours in advance.

- ½ cup of chopped green onions
- 1 cup of chopped green bell peppers
- 1 cup of chopped red bell peppers
- ¼ cup of sliced fresh or pickled jalapeños (optional)
- ½ cup of fresh lime juice
- ¼ cup of fresh lemon juice
- Salt and black pepper, to taste
- ½ tablespoon of finely chopped fresh dill (optional)
- 1 tablespoon of finely chopped parsley
- ½ tablespoon of finely chopped fresh tarragon (optional)
- 1 pound of fresh seafood, cut into bite-size chunks

Combine all of the ingredients in a large glass bowl or a plastic storage bag or container, then refrigerate.

Serve with crackers or in avocado halves.

Sugared Pecans

These are great to munch on during a sail or a cruise.

- 2 cups of sugar
- ¾ cup of milk
- 1 tablespoon of butter
- Pinch of salt
- 4 cups of pecan halves
- 1 teaspoon of vanilla

Combine the sugar, milk, butter and salt in a saucepan over medium heat and cook to the soft ball stage (234 to 240 on a candy thermometer). Add the pecans and vanilla and mix well.

Pour the mixture onto a sheet of wax or parchment paper and cool. Separate the pecans with a fork.

Store in an airtight container for up to one week.

SANDWICHES

Beef & Watercress Sandwiches

Makes 6 sandwiches

These sandwiches are great to take along on a day trip. Cook the beef a day in advance and store it in the refrigerator. Assemble the sandwiches before you depart and wrap them individually. Then, put the wrapped sandwiches in a large, shallow, airtight container and nestle it in the ice chest.

Take along some fruit (apples, berries, grapes) and store-bought or homemade cookies to satisfy your sweet tooth.

- 2 tablespoons of olive oil
- 1 ½ pounds of *filet mignon*, trimmed
- 1 pound of cream cheese, softened
- 5- to 6-inch piece of horseradish root, peeled and grated
- ⅓ cup of minced chives
- Salt and freshly ground black pepper, to taste
- 1 large bunch of watercress, stemmed
- 12 slices of firm whole wheat or country-style bread

Heat the oil in a large skillet over medium-high heat. Add the *filet mignon* and cook for four to five minutes on each side, or until the meat is medium-rare and browned on the outside. Remove from the pan and let stand for several minutes before slicing. Slice into thin pieces and set aside.

Combine the cream cheese, horseradish and chives. Mix well. Season with salt and pepper.

Spread each slice of bread with some of the cream cheese mixture. Top half of the slices with a few sprigs of the watercress. Arrange some slices of beef on top of the watercress, and cover with a few more sprigs of watercress. Top with the second slice of bread. Press gently to secure the ingredients. Serve at room temperature.

Roasted Vegetable Sandwiches

Makes 4 to 6 servings

Sometimes, vegetarian is good!

Roast the vegetables ahead of time and store them in plastic storage bags in the 'fridge or ice chest. Take them out and let them come to room temperature before making the sandwiches onboard.

- ¼ cup of red wine vinegar
- 2 tablespoons of olive oil
- ¼ cup of chopped fresh basil leaves
- 1 small eggplant, sliced into thin rounds
- 1 small zucchini, sliced into thin rounds
- 1 small yellow squash, sliced into thin rounds
- 1 medium-size red bell pepper, cut into thin strips
- 1 small red onion, thinly sliced
- Salt, freshly ground black pepper and cayenne, to taste
- Mayonnaise or yogurt
- 4 to 6 slices of toasted Italian bread

Preheat the oven to 450 degrees.

Combine the vinegar and oil in a large mixing bowl. Add the basil and the vegetables and toss to coat.

Spread the vegetables on a baking sheet or shallow roasting pan.

Bake, stirring occasionally, until the vegetables are tender and lightly browned, about 30 minutes. Remove from the oven and let cool.

Season the vegetables to taste.

Spread the mayonnaise or yogurt on the slices of bread and arrange the vegetables on the bread. Serve at room temperature.

Roquefort Burgers

Makes 6 to 8 servings

*There are times when nothing will satisfy me more than a
big burger stuffed with Roquefort cheese, so if you have a
grill, this is pretty simple to pull off.*

- 2 ½ pounds of ground sirloin
- ½ pound of ground chuck
- 1 ¼ teaspoons of salt
- ¾ teaspoon of freshly ground black pepper
- ¾ pound of Roquefort cheese, crumbled
- 8 hamburger buns, toasted
- Thinly sliced yellow onions (optional)

Combine the beef, salt and pepper and mix well.
Divide the mixture into six to eight equal portions.
Form into patties. Make a pocket in the center
of each patty and fill with the cheese. Cover the
cheese with the meat.

Heat a grill or skillet over high heat until very
hot. Lay the burgers in the pan without crowding
them. Reduce the heat to medium-high and cook
for four to five minutes. Flip the burgers and cook
until the meat feels firm, but gives slightly in the
center, about two minutes.

Serve on the buns, with the onions if you like.

Crabmeat Melt

My husband and I have been fortunate enough to be invited to join friends on their 95-foot Burger for cruises off the coast of Maine as well as in the Bahamas. The yacht is fully equipped and we always have a three-man crew. Captain Dick Peery's wife Karen is an incredible cook and does magic in her well-stocked galley. We've enjoyed everything from rack of lamb to lobster rolls and clam chowder, and her desserts are always incredible. She served us Crabmeat Melts for lunch one day on the aft deck, and she graciously gave me this recipe she got from her friend Barbara. It can be used for appetizers as well.

It's always best to use fresh lump crabmeat, but the canned product is quite acceptable.

- ¼ pound of margarine or butter
- 5-ounce jar of Kraft Old English Cheese
- 6 to 7 ounces of crabmeat (if canned, drain it well)
- 3 tablespoons of minced onions
- 2 tablespoons of chopped parsley
- ½ teaspoon of garlic powder
- 1 ½ tablespoons of mayonnaise
- 1 package (6-count) of English muffins, split into halves

Melt the butter and cheese in a medium-size saucepan over medium heat. Stir to blend and cook until the cheese is melted and the mixture is smooth.

Remove from the heat and add the next five ingredients.

Spread the mixture on the muffin halves. Place muffins in a single layer on a cookie sheet and freeze for about two hours.

Remove from freezer and store in an airtight container or plastic storage bag until ready to use. Keep frozen.

When ready to serve, **bake** on a cookie sheet at 350 degrees for about 15 minutes.

If you want to serve this as an appetizer, the English muffins can be cut into quarters before baking.

Mil's Mayonnaise

Makes about 1 quart

My friend Milou Simon Roy shared this recipe with me years ago. Make a batch to bring along for spreading on sandwiches, to dab on sliced tomatoes or cucumbers, or to serve with leftover cold chicken or beef.

- 1 onion, chopped
- 1 tablespoon of Worcestershire sauce
- 1 tablespoon of cayenne
- 1 tablespoon of black pepper
- 1 tablespoon of yellow mustard
- 1 tablespoon of lemon juice
- 1 tablespoon of ketchup
- 1 quart of mayonnaise

Put the first 7 ingredients in a blender and **pulse** several times to blend. Add the mayo and blend.

Store in an airtight container in the fridge.

Peppered Ham Salad

Makes about 3 cups

You can spread this on bread for sandwiches, or plop it on crackers to enjoy with a cold beverage for a snack. Keeps well in an airtight container.

- **3 cups of diced cooked ham**
- **¼ cup of minced green onions**
- **¼ cup of minced celery**
- **¼ cup of minced black olives**
- **2 tablespoons of minced pimento**
- **Mayonnaise, to taste**
- **1 tablespoon of Tabasco pepper sauce**
- **Freshly ground black pepper, to taste**
- **Worcestershire sauce, to taste**
- **Sliced rye or white bread**

Finely **chop** the ham in a food processor.

In a mixing bowl, **combine** the ham with the rest of the ingredients (except the bread).

Spread on bread slices for sandwiches.

Red Pepper Focaccia

Makes 12 servings

- 1 1/2 cups of warm water (about 110 degrees)
- 1 envelope (1/4 ounce) of dry yeast
- 1 teaspoon of sugar
- 3 3/4 cups (approximately) of all-purpose flour or 3 1/2 cups of bread flour
- 6 tablespoons of extra-virgin olive oil
- 1 1/2 teaspoons of salt
- 3 large red bell peppers, seeded and thinly sliced

In a large bowl, **combine** one-half cup of the warm water, the yeast, and the sugar. Stir to dissolve. Let stand for five minutes, or until foamy.

Add the remaining one cup of water, the flour, two tablespoons of the oil and the salt. Stir to combine.

Turn the dough onto a lightly floured surface and knead until smooth and elastic, about seven minutes. (Dough will be soft.)

Shape the dough into a ball. Lightly oil the inside of a large bowl. Add the dough and turn it to coat evenly with the oil.

Cover the bowl with plastic wrap or a clean towel and let it stand in a warm, draft-free place until it doubles in size, about one hour.

Lightly oil a 15½ x 10½-inch jelly roll pan. Punch the dough down and pat it into the prepared pan.

Cover and let rise in a warm place until it doubles in size, about 45 minutes.

With your fingertips, make deep indentations, about one inch apart, into the entire surface of the dough, nearly to the bottom of the pan. **Drizzle** with three tablespoons of the remaining olive oil.

Cover loosely and let rise in a warm place until it doubles in size, about 45 minutes.

Meanwhile, **heat** the remaining tablespoon of olive oil in a large skillet and add the red bell peppers. Cook, stirring frequently, for about 15 minutes. Season with salt and black pepper.

Preheat the oven to 450 degrees.

Spoon the peppers over the dough. **Bake** on the bottom rack until the bottom is crusty and the top is lightly browned, about 18 minutes.

Slide the focaccia from the pan onto a wire rack to cool.

SOUPS, SIDES & SALADS

Tomato Soup with Basil

Makes 6 servings

A great summertime soup! Make it in advance and store it in an airtight container to bring along to serve hot or cold!

- 1 teaspoon of olive oil
- 1 link of sweet or hot Italian sausage, removed from the casing and crumbled
- 1 large leek, white and pale green parts only, well rinsed and thinly sliced
- 1 teaspoon of minced garlic
- 1 medium rib of celery, thinly sliced
- 1 cup of chopped yellow onions
- Pinch or two of sugar
- 2 pounds of fresh, ripe tomatoes, peeled, seeded and chopped
- 3 cups of beef broth
- Salt and freshly ground black pepper, to taste
- 2 tablespoons of fresh lemon juice
- 6 tablespoons of finely chopped fresh basil leaves
- Tabasco pepper sauce, to taste (optional)

Heat the oil in a large soup pot over medium-high heat. Add the sausage and cook, stirring, until it is browned, about 10 minutes.

Add the leek, garlic, celery and onions and cook, stirring, until the vegetables are lightly golden, about 10 minutes.

Add the sugar, tomatoes and broth. Bring to a boil, then reduce the heat to medium-low. Cover and cook until the mixture thickens, about 30 minutes.

Remove the soup from the heat and let it cool for about 10 minutes.

Purée the soup in batches in a food processor or blender. Return it to the pot. Season with salt and pepper.

Heat the soup over medium heat. Add the lemon juice, four tablespoons of the basil and the Tabasco, if you wish.

When the soup has heated through, about five minutes, serve garnished with the remaining basil.

Gazpacho, My Way

Makes about 8 servings

This can be made ahead of time and stored in a glass or plastic container with a lid in the refrigerator or ice chest. It will last for about a week in the refrigerator, and it only gets better with time. The great plus here is that it's so healthy. I sometimes add a splash of ice cold vodka when serving and call it my Bloody Mary soup.

- 1 (46-ounce) can of tomato juice
- 4 large ripe tomatoes, chopped
- 1 medium-size green bell pepper, chopped
- 2 ribs of celery, chopped
- 1 medium-size sweet onion (such as a Vidalia or a Bermuda), chopped
- 3 tablespoons of chopped green onions
- 1 medium-size cucumber, peeled, seeded and chopped
- ½ teaspoon of minced garlic
- 1 tablespoon of finely chopped fresh basil leaves
- 1 tablespoon of finely chopped fresh cilantro leaves
- ½ teaspoon of salt (more or less, to taste)
- ¼ teaspoon of fresh ground black pepper (more or less, to taste)
- 2 tablespoons of extra-virgin olive oil (optional)

- 1 tablespoon of red wine vinegar
- 1 tablespoon of fresh lime juice
- 2 teaspoons of Worcestershire sauce
- ¼ teaspoon of Tabasco pepper sauce
  (more or less, to taste)

Combine all of the ingredients in a large bowl and stir to mix. If you wish to purée, do so in a food processor.

Cover and chill in the refrigerator for at least four hours before serving.

Tabbouleh

Makes 6 to 8 servings

I love this during the summer – it's refreshing and keeps well stored in the refrigerator or in an ice chest. You can add a couple of tablespoons of chopped fresh mint for an added zip!

- 1 cup of fine bulgur (No. 1)
- 1 1/3 cups of fresh lemon juice, (about five lemons)
- 3 bunches of green onions, trimmed and chopped
- 3 cups of chopped parsley (about 2 bunches)
- 3 large ripe tomatoes, chopped
- 1/3 cup of extra-virgin olive oil
- Salt and freshly ground black pepper

Put the bulgur into a large glass or ceramic dish and stir in one cup of the lemon juice and two cups of water. Cover the bowl and set aside at room temperature until most of the liquid has been absorbed and the bulgur is tender, about two hours.

Drain the bulgur in a sieve, gently pressing to remove excess liquid. Transfer it to a clean glass bowl and add the green onions, parsley, tomatoes, olive oil and the remaining ⅓ cup of lemon juice. Season to taste with salt and pepper, and stir to blend.

Store in an airtight container for up to 5 days.

Marinated Mixed Vegetables

Serves 6 to 8

So easy and so good! Make in advance and store the container with the marinated vegetables in an ice chest or refrigerator. This can be offered as a salad or side dish to sandwiches or grilled steaks.

- 3 cloves of garlic, crushed
- ¾ cup of olive oil
- 2 tablespoons of fresh lemon juice
- 2 tablespoons of red wine vinegar
- ¼ teaspoon of sugar
- 2 teaspoons of Dijon mustard
- Salt and freshly ground black pepper, to taste
- 1 small head of cauliflower, broken into florets
- 3 carrots, cut crosswise into ¼-inch slices
- 1 large green or red bell pepper, seeded and cut into strips
- ½ pound of green beans, trimmed and blanched in salted boiling water
- 1 large zucchini, cut into strips
- ½ pound of cherry tomatoes

Combine the garlic, oil, lemon juice, vinegar, sugar and Dijon mustard in a small bowl. Whisk to blend, then season with salt and black pepper.

Put the vegetables into a large shallow container fitted with a lid. Pour in the marinade and toss to coat evenly.

Cover with the lid and marinate for at least 24 hours, tossing the vegetables two to three times before serving.

Orzo Salad with Corn, Feta & Tomatoes

Makes about 8 servings

Store this in a large, wide-mouth jar or jug and nestle it in crushed ice before you leave the dock. This is a great lunch dish and, hey, you can add boiled shrimp or crabmeat to it when serving, if you like.

DRESSING
- 2 tablespoons of fresh lemon juice
- 1 tablespoon of olive oil
- 1 teaspoon of rice wine vinegar
- 1 teaspoon of Creole mustard
- 1/2 teaspoon of salt
- 1/4 teaspoon of freshly ground black pepper
- 3 cloves of garlic, crushed

SALAD
- 1 cup of uncooked orzo
- 2 cups of fresh yellow corn kernels (about 4 ears)
- 1 pint of cherry tomatoes, cut in half
- 1/2 cup of sliced red onions
- 1/2 cup of sliced black olives
- 1/2 cup of hearts of palm, cut crosswise into 1/2-inch pieces
- 1 cup of crumbled feta cheese

Combine the dressing ingredients in a jar and shake vigorously to blend.

Cook the orzo in a large pot of boiling salted water, stirring occasionally, about 8 minutes.

Add the corn and cook about 2 minutes more or until the pasta is still firm to the bite. Drain and place in a large bowl.

Add half the dressing and toss to coat. Cool a bit, then add the remaining ingredients and the rest of the dressing and toss to coat.

Cover and chill until ready to serve.

Shrimp & Rice Salad

Makes about 6 servings

Here is another make-ahead salad to store in airtight containers. I suggest serving this within 24 hours of making it as the rice tends to get soggy in the dressing mixture.

- 1 pound of medium shrimp, boiled, peeled and deveined
- 3 cups of cooked long-grain rice, at room temperature
- ¼ cup of chopped green olives
- ¼ cup of chopped celery
- 2 tablespoons of chopped green onions
- 2 tablespoons of chopped parsley
- Salt, cayenne and black pepper, to taste
- 1 hard-boiled egg, finely chopped
- 3 tablespoons of olive oil
- 1 tablespoon of cider vinegar
- 2 tablespoons of mayonnaise or sour cream

Combine all of the ingredients in a large bowl and toss to mix well. **Chill** for about 30 minutes before serving. The mixture can be stuffed into hollowed-out tomatoes if you like.

Beets & Onions

Makes 4 servings

Make this a day or so before you leave the dock. Store in wide-mouthed jars and keep chilled. Ideal as a salad.

- 1 (16-ounce) can of sliced beets, undrained
- ¼ cup of sugar
- 1 teaspoon of dry mustard
- ⅓ cup of cider vinegar
- 1 teaspoon of celery seeds
- 1 medium onion, thinly sliced
- ¼ teaspoon of salt (or more, to taste)
- ¼ teaspoon of freshly ground black pepper

Drain the beets, reserving the liquid.

Combine the beet liquid with the sugar, mustard, vinegar and celery seeds in a saucepan over medium heat. Stir to dissolve the sugar and mustard.

Add the onion, salt and black pepper and simmer for three to four minutes, or until the onion is slightly wilted. Remove from the heat.

Combine the mixture with the beets in a mixing bowl. Cool.

Cover and refrigerate for at least three hours (longer is better).

Garden Pesto

Makes about 2 cups

This pesto can be tossed with cooked pasta, spread on toast rounds or dabbed on sliced tomatoes. Make it ahead of time and store in an airtight container and keep chilled until ready to serve.

- 3 cups of fresh basil (tightly packed), gently rinsed and patted dry
- 5 cloves of garlic
- 1/2 cup of toasted pine nuts (or walnuts or pecans)
- 1/2 cup of freshly grated Parmesan cheese
- 2 tablespoons of freshly grated Pecorino Romano cheese
- 2/3 cup of virgin olive oil
- Salt and freshly ground black pepper, to taste

In a food processor, **combine** the basil and garlic and pulse two or three times to chop. Add the nuts and cheeses, and pulse once or twice.

Slowly **add** the oil and blend. Season with salt and pepper.

The mixture can be stored in the refrigerator in airtight containers for a week or so.

Fruit Compote

Makes 4 servings

Easy, easy! If you have fresh fruit, by all means use that, but this is quite good made with canned fruits. You can also add dried cranberries!

- 1 (10-ounce) can of mandarin oranges, drained
- 1 (10-ounce) can of grapefruit sections, drained
- 1 (20-ounce) can of pineapple chunks, drained
- 1 tablespoon of sugar or sugar substitute
- Fresh mint leaves (optional)

Combine the fruit and the sugar in an airtight container and tuck in several mint leaves if available. If not, use some dried mint, to taste.

Chill before serving.

MAIN COURSES

FOR THOSE WHO LOVE TO GRILL

If your boat is equipped with a small grill, by all means pack a couple of steaks in your refrigerator or ice chest. You can also purchase pre-made kabobs at some markets, and these are easily packed to store onboard.

There are many marinades on the market, but I make one (in a jar fitted with a lid) with two parts olive oil, one part soy sauce and one part Cajun Power Garlic Sauce, to have on hand.

Grilled Steaks with Onions & Peppers

Makes 4 servings

- 1 tablespoon of vegetable oil
- 1 yellow onion, cut in half then thinly sliced
- 1 red bell pepper, cored, seeded and cut into thin strips
- 2 tablespoons of Creole mustard
- Salt and freshly ground black pepper, to taste
- 4 beef tenderloin fillets, each about 6 ounces, about 1 inch thick

Prepare a charcoal fire or gas grill.

Heat two teaspoons of the oil in a large skillet over medium heat. Add the onions and peppers and sauté for about five minutes, or until soft.

In a small bowl, **whisk** the mustard with ¼ cup of water, add this to the onion mixture and cook until most of the liquid has evaporated, about two minutes. Season with salt and pepper. Keep warm.

Brush the steaks lightly with the remaining oil and season to taste with salt and black pepper.

Grill the steaks to desired doneness, about three to four minutes per side for medium-rare.

To serve, **spoon** the onion mixture over the steaks.

Squash &
Pepper Kabobs

Makes 4 servings

- 1 ½ pounds of yellow squash (or zucchini)
- 1 medium green bell pepper
- 1 medium red bell pepper
- ⅓ cup of olive oil
- 2 tablespoons of red wine vinegar
- 1 clove of garlic, minced
- 2 teaspoons of chopped fresh thyme
  or ½ teaspoon of dried thyme
- ½ teaspoon of salt
- ¼ teaspoon of freshly ground black pepper
- 10 to 12 large button mushrooms, cleaned
  and stemmed

Cut the squash (or zucchini) crosswise into one-inch slices.

Halve the green and red bell peppers and remove the seeds and stems. Cut the peppers into one-inch squares.

In a large bowl, **whisk** together the oil, vinegar, garlic, thyme, salt and pepper.

Add the vegetables and toss to coat evenly. Let stand for about 30 minutes.

Prepare the grill. Remove the vegetables from the marinade; reserve the marinade.

Thread the pepper, squash pieces and mushrooms alternately onto skewers. Arrange the skewers on the rack.

Grill, turning occasionally and brushing with the reserved marinade, until lightly browned, for about 8 to 10 minutes.

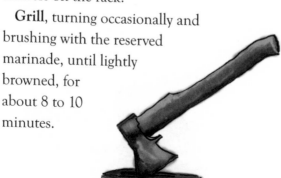

Shrimp & Garlic Kabobs

Makes 4 to 6 servings

- 12 to 16 large garlic cloves, peeled
- 1/3 cup of olive oil
- 1/4 cup of tomato sauce
- 2 tablespoons of red wine vinegar
- 2 tablespoons of chopped fresh basil or 1 1/2 teaspoons of dried basil
- 2 teaspoons of minced garlic
- 1/2 teaspoon of salt
- 1/2 teaspoon of cayenne
- 1/4 teaspoon of freshly ground black pepper
- Pinch of sugar
- 2 pounds of large shrimp, peeled and deveined (leave the tails on)

Drop the whole garlic cloves into boiling water and boil for about three minutes. Drain and set aside.

Combine the olive oil, tomato sauce, vinegar, basil, minced garlic, salt, cayenne, black pepper and sugar in a large bowl and stir to mix well. Add the shrimp and toss to coat evenly. Cover and refrigerate for 30 minutes.

Remove the shrimp from the marinade and reserve the marinade left in the bowl.

Thread the shrimp and whole garlic cloves alternately on skewers. Put the skewers on the grill. (If you prefer, the kabobs can be arranged in a wire grill rack or basket.)

Grill, turning them several times and brushing them with the reserved marinade for six to eight minutes, or until the shrimp turn pink.

Beef Kabobs

Makes about 8 servings

You can pick up pre-made beef (and chicken) kabobs at some supermarkets, but you can also make them yourself.

- 1 sirloin steak, about 1 ½ pounds, about 1 inch thick, cut into 2-inch cubes
- 1 tablespoon of Cajun or Creole seasoning mix
- 2 tablespoons of balsamic vinegar
- 1 tablespoon of yellow mustard
- 2 tablespoons of Worcestershire sauce
- 1 teaspoon of fresh lemon juice
- 1 teaspoon of garlic powder
- 1 large red bell pepper, cut into 2-inch pieces
- 1 large green bell pepper, cut into 2-inch pieces
- 1 large purple onion, cut into 2-inch pieces

Put the meat into a shallow bowl. Make a marinade by combining the seasoning mix, vinegar, mustard, Worcestershire sauce, lemon juice and garlic powder in a small bowl and pour it over the meat. Let it sit, covered, in the refrigerator for at least 2 hours.

Remove the meat from the marinade. Thread the meat and vegetables alternately on double bamboo skewers (soaked in water for about one hour before using).

Place the kabobs on the grill, close the lid and cook for 10 minutes. Turn, close the lid again and cook for 10 minutes. Turn again, close the lid and cook for 15 minutes more – a total of about 35 minutes.

Grilled Salmon and/or Tuna with Anchovy Butter

Makes about 6 servings

If you can find salmon or tuna (or perhaps you'll bring in a yellowfin tuna on a fishing trip), this is delicious. You can also use any firm, white fish for this preparation. Just be sure the fish is fresh, fresh, fresh!

- 1 pound of fresh tuna fillets
- 1 pound of fresh salmon fillets
- 2 tablespoons plus ¼ cup of olive oil
- Salt and freshly ground black pepper, to taste
- 3 medium-size yellow onions, peeled and cut into ¼-inch slices
- 6 to 8 anchovy fillets (packed in oil and drained)
- 6 tablespoons of butter, softened
- 1 ½ tablespoons of fresh lemon juice
- 2 teaspoons soy sauce

Prepare the grill.

Rub the tuna and salmon with two tablespoons of the olive oil, then season them generously with salt and pepper.

Put the onion slices in a bowl with the remaining ¼ cup of olive oil and toss to coat evenly. Season with salt and pepper. Set aside.

Put the anchovies in a small bowl and mash with a fork. Add the butter, lemon juice and soy, then season with salt and pepper. Blend well.

Grill the fish for about two minutes on each side (don't overcook), and grill the onions for about a minute on each side.

To **serve**, separate the onion slices into rings and scatter them over the tuna and salmon. Smear the anchovy butter over the fish and onions. Serve warm.

Herbed Butter

If you have a grill onboard or have access to a grill, this compound butter is great to put on steaks or seafood when they come hot off the grill. Keep the butter chilled and simply put a couple of chunks on the hot food. Oh, you can also put it on warm grilled vegetables.

- **2 sticks of butter, at room temperature**
- **1 teaspoon each of finely chopped fresh parsley leaves, sage, oregano and rosemary**
- **Freshly ground black pepper, to taste**

Beat the butter until creamy. Add the herbs and beat again.

Roll into cylinders and cover with plastic wrap, or spoon the mixture into crocks, small ramekins or jars.

Cover with plastic wrap and refrigerate.

Alternatives: To make basil butter, add two to three teaspoons of finely chopped fresh basil leaves to the butter. For garlic butter, add two tablespoons of minced garlic.

Sausages with Aioli

Makes about 12 appetizer portions

Cook your choice of sausages before leaving home and pack them in plastic storage bags. Make the aioli and store it in a jar fitted with a lid. Put all in the ice chest. This makes a great appetizer, but it can also be the main course for a quick supper. Serve it with Marinated Mixed Vegetables. (See recipe on page 86.)

- ¾ cup of good-quality mayonnaise
- ½ teaspoon of coarsely ground black pepper
- 2 medium-size garlic cloves, pressed
- 2 pounds of assorted cooked sausages, such as smoked pork, Italian and fresh pork
- Several sprigs of fresh oregano or rosemary
- Thinly sliced Italian bread

To make the aioli, **combine** the mayonnaise, black pepper and garlic in a small bowl and mix well. Refrigerate for at least one hour.

Cut the sausages crosswise into bite-size pieces. Arrange them on a platter lined with the fresh oregano or rosemary. Serve with the aioli and bread.

Linguine with Peppery White Clam Sauce

Makes 4 servings

Talk about easy! If your vessel has a butane cook-top, make this for a quick supper.

- ¼ cup of olive oil
- 2 garlic cloves, crushed or minced
- ¼ teaspoon of crushed dried red pepper or a pinch of cayenne
- 1 (10 ½-ounce) can of chopped clams with juice
- 1 pound of linguini
- ¼ cup of pasta cooking liquid
- 3 tablespoons of fresh lemon juice
- 2 tablespoons of chopped fresh parsley
- Coarsely ground black pepper

Heat the oil in a skillet over low heat. Stir in the garlic and cook, stirring, over low heat for about two minutes (do not brown). Add the red pepper or cayenne and cook, stirring, for one minute.

Add the clams with their juice and simmer, uncovered, for about 10 minutes.

Cook the linguini until tender, then drain, reserving ¼ cup of the cooking liquid.

Toss the linguine with the clam sauce, pasta cooking liquid, lemon juice and parsley. Sprinkle with black pepper. Serve immediately.

No-Cook Tomato Sauce

Makes about 2 cups

This is another pasta sauce made with fresh tomatoes rather than canned ones. If you can bring fresh tomatoes with you, or happen upon a farmers' market near where your boat docks, this is the way to go.

- 3 to 4 large ripe tomatoes, peeled, seeded and chopped
- 1/3 cup of cured olives (optional)
- 2 teaspoons of finely chopped garlic
- Salt and freshly ground black pepper, to taste
- 1/3 cup of extra-virgin olive oil
- 1/4 cup of chopped fresh parsley leaves
- 1/4 cup of chopped fresh basil leaves
- Cooked pasta
- Freshly grated Parmesan cheese for garnish

In a large bowl, **combine** the tomatoes, olives, garlic, salt and pepper. Whisk in the olive oil, then add the parsley and basil.

If you prefer a smoother sauce, **pulse** all these ingredients in a food processor to desired consistency.

To **serve,** toss the tomato sauce with pasta and top with Parmesan cheese.

Summer Spaghetti

Makes 4 servings

This can be prepared ahead of time. Put the tomato mixture in one airtight container or plastic storage bag and put the cooked pasta in another. Keep chilled, but bring to room temperature before serving. Don't forget to pack a small container of grated Parmesan cheese!

Check out your grocery shelves for a variety of canned diced tomatoes. Some are flavored with basil and others with garlic. Find one that suits your taste.

- 2 (14.5-ounce) cans of diced tomatoes
- ½ cup of chopped tomatoes
- 1 tablespoon of minced garlic
- 2 tablespoons of minced parsley
- ½ teaspoon of dried basil leaves
- ¼ cup of olive oil
- 1 teaspoon of tarragon vinegar
- Salt and black pepper, to taste
- ½ pound of thin spaghetti
- 1 tablespoon of olive oil
- Grated Parmesan cheese for serving

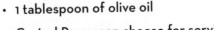

Combine the tomatoes, garlic, parsley, basil, olive oil and tarragon vinegar and toss to mix.

Season with salt and pepper and store in an airtight container and keep chilled.

Cook the pasta until *al dente*. Drain and rinse in cool water.

Allow to cool for about 10 minutes before tossing with the olive oil.

Store in an airtight container or plastic storage bags and chill.

Serve with grated Parmesan cheese.

Meat Loaf with Roquefort

Makes about 6 to 8 servings

Make a meat loaf ahead of time to bring along to make sandwiches. Easy and delicious. Just remember to cool the meat loaf completely before wrapping securely in foil and plastic wrap to store in the refrigerator.

- 1 pound of ground chuck
- 1/2 pound of lean ground pork
- 1/2 pound of ground veal
- 1/2 cup of finely chopped onion
- 2 cups of bread crumbs
- 1/2 cup of chopped parsley
- 1/4 cup of ketchup
- 1 tablespoon of Creole mustard
- 2 eggs, beaten
- 1 1/2 teaspoons of salt
- 1/4 teaspoon of cayenne
- 1/4 teaspoon of freshly ground black pepper
- 1/2 pound of crumbled Roquefort cheese
- 1/2 cup of chopped black olives

Combine the chuck, pork, veal, onions, bread crumbs, parsley, ketchup, mustard, eggs, salt, cayenne and black pepper in a large mixing bowl. Mix well, but do not over work.

Form the mixture into a large loaf and place in a lightly greased baking pan. Using your fingers, make a deep groove down the center of the loaf, from end to end, and about two inches deep.

Combine the cheese and the olives and spread this mixture evenly in the opening. Pinch the meat mixture to close over the cheese mixture.

Bake at 375 degrees for about one hour, or until the juices run clear.

Remove from the oven and let sit for about five minutes before slicing to serve.

Italian Meat Loaf

Makes 8 to 10 servings

- 1 pound of ground chuck
- ½ pound of lean ground pork
- ½ pound of ground veal
- 1 pound of Italian sausage, removed from the casing and crumbled
- ½ cup of finely chopped onion
- 1 tablespoon of finely chopped garlic
- 3 cups of bread crumbs
- 3 tablespoons of chopped parsley
- 2 teaspoon of salt
- 1 teaspoon of cayenne
- ½ teaspoon of freshly ground black pepper
- 1 teaspoon of dried basil leaves
- 1 teaspoon of dried oregano leaves
- 2 eggs, lightly beaten
- ½ cup of tomato sauce
- ½ cup of dry red wine
- ½ cup of chopped green olives
- 1 cup of grated mozzarella

Combine all of the ingredients except the mozzarella in a large mixing bowl. Mix well, but do not over work.

Form the mixture into a large loaf and place it in a large, lightly greased baking pan.

Bake uncovered at 375 degrees for about one hour or until the juices run clear.

Sprinkle the top with the cheese. Bake for about five minutes more or until the cheese melts.

Remove loaf from the oven and let it stand for about 10 minutes before slicing. It can also be served at room temperature or chilled.

Serve with lots of crusty Italian bread.

Southwestern Chili-Cheese Meat Loaf

Makes 6 to 8 servings

- ¼ cup of olive oil
- 1 cup of chopped onions
- ½ cup of chopped red bell peppers
- 4 garlic cloves, minced
- 2 fresh jalapeños, seeded and minced
- 2 tablespoons of chili powder
- 2 tablespoons of salt
- 2 teaspoons of dried leaf oregano
- 2 teaspoons of ground cumin
- 1 (28-ounce) can of Italian peeled tomatoes, crushed and drained
- 1 ½ pounds of ground beef
- ½ pound of lean ground pork
- 1 cup of fine bread crumbs
- 2 large eggs, beaten
- 1 cup of corn kernels, canned or frozen
- 3 green onions, thinly sliced
- ½ pound of sharp Cheddar cheese

Heat the olive oil in a large skillet over high heat. Add the onions, bell peppers, garlic, jalapeño peppers, chili powder, salt, oregano and cumin. Cover, reduce the heat to low and cook, stirring once or twice, until the vegetables are soft, about 10 minutes.

Add the tomatoes and cook, covered, stirring once or twice, for 10 minutes longer. Remove from the heat and cool to room temperature.

Preheat the oven to 350 degrees.

Combine the beef and pork in a large bowl. Add the tomato mixture, bread crumbs and eggs. Mix well. Add the corn and green onions, then mix again. Transfer the mixture to a shallow baking dish or pan and form into a flat loaf.

Bake uncovered for about one hour, or until the juices run clear. Pour off any grease and pan juices that have accumulated in the bottom of the pan.

Sprinkle meat loaf with the cheese, return loaf to the oven, and bake until the cheese is melted, about four minutes.

DESSERTS

Lemon–Lime Pound Cake

Makes 10 to 12 servings

- 2 sticks (1/2 pound) of unsalted butter, at room temperature
- 2 cups of sugar, divided
- 5 eggs, at room temperature
- 1 tablespoon of grated lemon zest
- 1 tablespoon of grated lime zest
- 2 cups of sifted all-purpose flour
- 1/2 teaspoon of salt
- 1/4 teaspoon of baking powder
- 1 1/2 tablespoons of fresh lemon juice
- 1 1/2 tablespoons of fresh lime juice

Preheat the oven to 325 degrees. Butter and lightly dust with flour a 9x5x3-inch loaf pan.

In a mixing bowl, **cream** the butter until smooth. Gradually add 1½ cups of the sugar and beat until the mixture is light and fluffy, about five minutes.

Add the eggs, one at a time, beating well after each addition. Beat in the lemon and lime zests.

Sift together the flour, salt and baking powder.

Add the dry ingredients, about ½ cup at a time, to the butter mixture, beating on low speed until all is blended. Spoon the batter into the pan.

Bake for 1 hour and 15 minutes or until the edges of the cake pull slightly away from the pan and the top springs back when touched. Cool the cake in the pan on a wire rack for about five minutes.

To make a citrus glaze, **combine** the remaining ½ cup of sugar and the lemon and lime juice in a small nonreactive saucepan. Cook over medium heat, stirring to dissolve the sugar, for one to two minutes. Do not boil. Remove from the heat.

Invert the pan to unmold the cake over a sheet of waxed paper.

While the cake is still warm, **brush** it all over with the hot citrus glaze.

Let it **cool** completely, then wrap it in plastic wrap then in foil.

Let it **stand** for at least one day before slicing. It will keep for one week.

Sour Cream Pound Cake

Makes 8 to 10 servings

I'm a big fan of pound cakes. Once they are baked, they can be wrapped and stored in plastic storage bags.

Rinse blueberries, pat them dry and then put them in an airtight container with a splash of brandy to bring along (in the ice chest) to serve with the pound cake.

- 1 stick of butter, softened
- 1 cup of sugar
- 3 eggs
- 1 ¼ cups of all-purpose flour
- 1 teaspoon of baking soda
- 1 teaspoon of ground cinnamon
- 1 cup of sour cream
- 1 teaspoon of vanilla extract

Preheat the oven to 350 degrees. Lightly grease a loaf pan and lightly dust the pan with flour; set aside.

Cream the butter and sugar together in a bowl until the mixture is light and fluffy. Beat in the eggs one at a time.

Sift the flour with the baking soda and cinnamon and stir half of the dry ingredients into the batter. Beat in the sour cream and the vanilla, then stir in the rest of the dry ingredients.

Pour the mixture into the pan and rap the pan sharply on the table to remove any air pockets. Bake for about one hour, until the top of the cake is golden brown and lightly spongy to the touch. Remove from the oven and cool before removing from the pan.

Wrap the pound cake in plastic wrap and then in foil to keep it fresh.

Fig Cake

Makes 1 cake to serve about 12 slices

If you have fig preserves in your pantry, this is a cake for you! Once it's baked and cooled, it can be wrapped securely in plastic wrap and foil. Great for dessert or breakfast.

- **2 cups of sugar**
- **3 large eggs**
- **1 cup of vegetable oil**
- **1 cup of whole milk**
- **2 cups of bleached all-purpose flour**
- **2 teaspoons of ground cinnamon**
- **1 teaspoon of salt**
- **1 teaspoon of baking soda**
- **1 cup of pecan pieces**
- **2 cups of mashed fig preserves**

Preheat the oven to 350 degrees.

Cream the sugar and the eggs. Add the vegetable oil and stir well to blend. Add the milk and mix well.

In a separate bowl, **combine** the flour, cinnamon, salt and baking soda. Mix well. Add this mixture to the first mixture, stirring, to blend.

Add the pecans and figs. Stir again to blend.

Pour mixture into a 12-cup bundt pan and bake until it sets, about one hour.

Remove and cool before slicing to serve.

Classic Chess Pie

Makes 1 pie (serves 6 to 8)

This is an old-time Southern favorite and can be made either in a regular pie pan or a 6-inch square pan. Once the pie is cooked and cooled, it can be cut into wedges or squares and packed in an airtight container for traveling.

- 3 cups of sugar
- 1 stick of butter or margarine, softened
- 5 eggs, lightly beaten
- 3 tablespoons of cornmeal
- 2 teaspoons of pure vanilla extract
- 1/8 teaspoon of salt
- 1 cup of milk
- 1 unbaked 9-inch pie shell

Preheat the oven to 325 degrees.

Combine the sugar and butter in a mixing bowl. Beat at low speed with an electric mixer until blended.

Beat in the eggs, cornmeal, vanilla and salt. Add the milk. Beat at low speed until blended.

Pour the mixture into the pie shell.

Bake at 325 degrees for about one hour to one hour and 15 minutes or until the filling sets. Cover the edge of the pie with foil if necessary to prevent overbrowning.

Cool to room temperature before serving.

Chocolate Mint Cookies

Makes about 3 1/2 dozen

Store-bought cookies are perfectly acceptable to take along on outings, but if you have the time, make these for a special treat.

- 2/3 cup of butter or margarine
- 1 cup of sugar
- 1/3 cup of firmly packed dark brown sugar
- 1 large egg
- 1 teaspoon of pure vanilla extract
- 1 ounce of square unsweetened chocolate, melted
- 1 1/2 cups of all-purpose flour
- 10 ounces of mint chocolate morsels

Preheat the oven to 325 degrees.

Beat the butter at medium speed with an electric mixer until fluffy. Gradually add the sugars, beating well. Add the egg, vanilla and melted chocolate, mixing well.

Gradually **add** the flour, mixing well. Stir in the mint chocolate morsels.

Drop by the level tablespoonful onto a lightly greased cookie sheet.

Bake for 12 to 15 minutes.

Cool on the cookie sheet for about three minutes, then transfer cookies to a wire rack to cool before storing them in an airtight container.

Pecan Cookies

Makes about 3 dozen

- ½ cup of butter
- ¾ cup of firmly packed brown sugar
- 1 egg, beaten
- 1 ¼ cups of all-purpose flour
- ½ teaspoon of baking soda
- ½ teaspoon of salt
- 1 teaspoon of vanilla extract
- ½ cup of pecans (or walnuts), coarsely chopped

Preheat the oven to 375 degrees. Grease two baking sheets.

Cream the butter and sugar together. Add the egg and mix well. Sift together the flour, soda and salt and add to the butter mixture. Add the vanilla and one teaspoon of hot water and mix. Add the pecans and mix again.

Drop by the rounded teaspoonful onto the cookie sheets.

Bake until golden brown, about 12 minutes.

Transfer to a wire rack to cool. Store in an airtight container.

Index of Recipes
– Alphabetical –

Index of Recipes
– By Food Category –

Beef

Bread

Cake

Cheese

Cookies

Eggs

Misc.
Fruit Compote, 93
Mil's Mayonnaise, 74
Pico de Gallo, 52
Sugared Pecans, 64
Tabbouleh, 84

Pork
Italian Meat Loaf, 116
Meat Loaf with Roquefort, 114
Peppered Ham Salad, 75
Sausage-Stuffed Loaves, 60
Sausages with Aioli, 107
Southern Sausage Cake, 28
Southwestern Chili-Cheese Meat Loaf, 118

Poultry
Chicken Liver *Paté*, 44

Sauces
Garden Pesto, 92
Herbed Butter, 106
Jezebel Sauce (No. 1), 56
Jezebel Sauce (No. 2), 57
No-Cook Tomato Sauce, 110

Seafood
Ceviche, 62
Crabmeat Melt, 72
Grilled Salmon and/or Tuna with Anchovy Butter, 104
Linguine with Peppery White Clam Sauce, 108
Marinated Shrimp & Corn, 42
Seafood Spread, 46
Shrimp & Garlic Kabobs, 100
Shrimp & Rice Salad, 90
Smoked Oyster Log, 51

Vegetables

About the author...

MARCELLE BIENVENU is a cookbook author and food writer who has been preparing Cajun and Creole dishes since the 1960s. She is currently a chef/instructor at the John Folse Culinary Institute at Nicholls State University in Thibodaux, Louisiana.

A native of St. Martinville, La., in the heart of the Cajun country, she has written a weekly food column, "Creole Cooking," for *The Times-Picayune* of New Orleans since 1984. She's worked as a researcher and consultant for Time-Life Books, contributing to a series of books titled *Foods of the World*. She's been featured in *Food & Wine, Southern Living, Redbook, The New York Times, Louisiana Life, Louisiana Cookin'* and *Acadiana Profile*.

She is the author of four cookbooks: *Who's Your Mama, Are You Catholic and Can You Make a Roux? (Book 1), Who's Your Mama...? (Book 2), Cajun Cooking for Beginners,* and *No Baloney On My Boat!*

She co-authored four cookbooks with renowned chef Emeril Lagasse. She also co-authored *Eula Mae's Cajun Kitchen* with Eula Mae Doré, a longtime cook for the McIlhenny family on Avery Island, and *Stir the Pot: The History of Cajun Cuisine*, with Carl A. Brasseaux and Ryan A. Brasseaux.

With Judy Walker, food editor for *The Times-Picayune*, Ms. Bienvenu co-authored *Cooking Up A Storm: Recipes Lost and Found from The Times-Picayune of New Orleans*, which was nominated for a James Beard Award in 2009.

She also co-authored *Wings of Paradise: Birds of the Louisiana Wetlands* with Charlie Hohorst, as well as *Pecans: From Soups to Nuts.*

She owned and operated a restaurant, Chez Marcelle, near Lafayette, La., in the early 1980s, and has worked for several restaurants, including Commander's Palace and K-Paul's Louisiana Kitchen in New Orleans.

A graduate of the University of Southwestern Louisiana, she lives on Bayou Teche in St. Martinville, La., with her husband, Rock Lasserre.

Cookbooks by
Acadian House Publishing
The Nation's leading publisher of authentic Cajun and Creole recipes

No Baloney On My Boat!

A cookbook filled with dozens of recipes for tasty and nutritious foods that can be prepared in advance for outdoor adventures. It's a small cookbook, portable, easy to carry around and filled with simple recipes. And the baloney sandwich isn't one of them! It contains recipes for summer spaghetti, antipasto salad, marinated shrimp & corn, grilled tuna and other nutritious foods. (Author: Marcelle Bienvenu. ISBN: 0-925417-69-6. Price: $17.95)

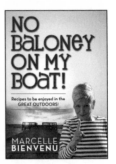

Cajun Cooking For Beginners

A 48-page saddle-stitched soft cover book that teaches the basics of authentic Cajun cooking. It contains about 50 simple, easy-to-follow recipes; cooking tips and hints; a glossary of Cajun food terms, such as roux, gumbo, jambalaya and *etouffee*; and definitions of basic cooking terms, such as beat, blend, broil, sauté and simmer. (Author: Marcelle Bienvenu. ISBN: 0-925417-23-8. Price: $7.95)

MARCELLE BIENVENU

Cajun Cooking (Book 1)

...contains about 400 of the best Cajun recipes, like Jambalaya, Crawfish Pie, Filé Gumbo, *Cochon de Lait*, Chicken & Okra Gumbo, *Sauce Piquante*. Special features include a section on homemade baby foods and drawings of classic south Louisiana scenery. (ISBN: 0-925417-03-3. Price: $17.95)

Who's Your Mama, Are You Catholic, and Can You Make A Roux? (Book 1)

A 160-page hardcover book containing more than 200 Cajun and Creole recipes, plus old photos and interesting stories about the author's growing up in the Cajun country of south Louisiana. Recipes include *Pain Perdu*, *Couche Couche*, Chicken *Fricassée*, Stuffed Mirliton, Shrimp Stew, *Grillades*, Red Beans & Rice, Shrimp Creole, *Bouillabaisse*, Pralines. (Author: Marcelle Bienvenu. ISBN 0-925417-55-6. Price: $22.95)

Who's Your Mama, Are You Catholic, and Can You Make A Roux? (Book 2)

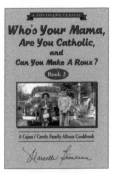

A 104-page hardcover book containing about 100 Cajun and Creole recipes, plus old photos and interesting stories about the author's growing up in the Cajun country of south Louisiana. Recipes include Shrimp Bisque, Andouille & Black Bean Soup, Crawfish-Okra Gumbo, Smothered Okra, Stuffed Tomatoes, Eggplant & Rice Dressing, Stuffed Pork Chops, Chicken & Oyster Pie, Apple Cake, Roasted Pecans. (Author: Marcelle Bienvenu. ISBN 0-925417-59-9. Price: $17.95)

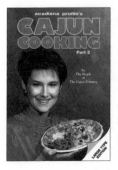

Cajun Cooking (Book 2)

...picks up where Part 1 left off. It contains such delicious dishes as Shrimp & Crab Bisque, Fresh Vegetable Soup, Seafood-Stuffed Bellpepper, Broiled Seafood Platter, Yam-Pecan Cake. The recipes appear in the same easy-to-follow format as in Part 1, except they're in real large print for an arm's-length reading. (ISBN: 0-925417-05-X. Price: $15.95)

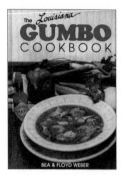

The Louisiana GUMBO Cookbook

A 192-page hardcover book with more than 100 recipes for the Cajun and Creole gumbo dishes that have made south Louisiana food world-famous. Special sections on the history of gumbo and filé, plus instructions for making rice and gumbo stocks. (Authors: Bea & Floyd Weber. ISBN: 0-925417-13-0. Price: $19.95)

The Top 100 NEW ORLEANS Recipes Of All Time

A 192-page hardcover book containing 100 of the recipes that have helped to make New Orleans food world-famous. For example, Shrimp Creole, Red Beans & Rice, Blackened Redfish, Oyster Loaf, Muffaletta, *Beignets, Café au Lait* and King Cake. (ISBN: 0-925417-51-3. Price: $16.95)

The Top 100 CAJUN Recipes Of All Time

A 160-page hardcover book containing 100 recipes selected by the editors of *Acadiana Profile*, "The Magazine of the Cajun Country." For example, *Boudin, Couche Couche, Maque Choux*, Mirliton, Crawfish *Etouffee*, Chicken *Fricassee*, Pralines—the classics of South Louisiana cuisine. (Hardcover ISBN: 0-925417-52-1, Price $16.95; Softcover, 7x10 size with 48 pages, ISBN: 0-925417-20-3, Price: $7.95)

TO ORDER, list the books you wish to purchase along with the corresponding cost of each. Add shipping & handling cost of $3 for the first book and 75¢ per book thereafter. Louisiana residents add 8% tax to the cost of the books. Mail your order and check or credit card authorization (VISA/MC/AmEx) to: Acadian House Publishing, Dept. BAL, P.O. Box 52247, Lafayette, LA 70505. Or call (800) 850-8851. Or order online, www.acadianhouse.com.